AF358470

The Ultimate *Jaguar* Book for Kids

100+ Amazing Jaguar Facts, Photos & More

Jenny Kellett

Copyright © 2026 Bellanova Books

Jaguars: The Ultimate Jaguar Book
www.bellanovabooks.com

ISBN: 978-619-7695-08-3

Contents

Introduction

Jaguars have fascinated American civilizations for thousands of years. Their beautiful spotted coats and physical prowess make them one of the world's most inspiring big cats.

In this book, you'll learn more about the daily lives of jaguars, what makes them so unique, and the problems they face. At the end, test your knowledge in our jaguar quiz.

Are you ready? *Let's go!*

The range of jaguars, now (dark blue) and in the past (light blue).

© IUCN

Jaguars: The Basics

What are jaguars and where do they live?

The scientific name for the jaguar is *Panthera onca*.

• • •

Jaguars are part of the *Panthera* genus, which is part of the bigger *Felidae* family. There are five species in the *Panthera* genus, also known as the **"Big Cats"**: lion (*Panthera leo*), leopard (*Panthera pardus*), Jaguar (*Panthera onca*), snow leopard (*Panthera uncia*), and tiger (*Panthera tigris*).

Today, there are no subspecies of the jaguar. However, before 2017 scientists believed there were nine subspecies.

• • •

Although there are no subspecies of jaguars anymore, biologists divide them up into four regional groups: Mexico and Guatemala; north of the Amazon; south of the Amazon; and southern Central America.

Jaguars differ slightly in size and appearance in each of these groups—with those living further north generally smaller than those in the south.

A jaguar in Brazil   >

Nobody knows the exact number of jaguars living in the wild, but the WWF estimates that there are around 173,000.

. . .

Jaguars live across much of the Americas, from the southwestern United States down to northern Argentina. Some of the countries they live in include Belize, Guatemala, Honduras, Nicaragua, Brazil, Paraguay and Venezuela. They are believed to be extinct in El Salvador and Uruguay.

. . .

Sadly, the jaguar only lives in around 55 per cent of its historic range.

The jaguar used to be quite common in the
southern United States, including in Colorado
and Louisiana. However, since 1900 it has
been almost extinct there.

. . .

Jaguars are big cats! In fact, they are the
largest species of cat living in the Americas
and the third largest cat species in the
world—only the lion and the tiger are larger.

. . .

Jaguars are very adaptable to their
environment and live in a wide range
of habitats including wetlands, tropical
rainforests, wooded areas and more.

In the past, when jaguars lived in the United States, they liked to live in dense oak forests.

• • •

The word "jaguar" is believed to come from the Mesoamerican word ""yaguar", which means "to kill with one leap".

<   **A jaguar in Pantanal, Brazil.**

If you live in North America, you probably pronounce 'jaguar' with two syllables (jag-uar), while in British English it is pronounced with three syllables (jag-u-ar)!

. . .

In many areas, the jaguar and the cougar have the same range and compete for the same food (they are **sympatric**).

. . .

Male and female jaguars don't have special names like many other species, they are simply 'male jaguar' and 'female jaguar'!

A female jaguar in Costa Rica >

Jaguar Characteristics

Size, features, special traits and more.

Jaguars are **apex predators**, meaning they are at the top of the food chain in their habitats and don't have any of their own predators.

• • •

The jaguar's weight range is huge: they vary from 56-96 kg (123-212 lb). The largest males can weigh as much as 158 kg (348 lb), and the smallest females weigh around 36 kg (79 lb).

An adult female jaguar.

Female jaguars are usually 10-20 per cent smaller than males.

• • •

Jaguars can be up to 170 cm (5'6") long, not including their long tails, which are up to 80 cm (2'6") long.

• • •

Jaguars have excellent night vision and their eyes are adapted for night hunting. Like other cats, jaguars have a unique mirror-like structure at the back of their eyes, which reflects light back into their retina to improve their night vision. If you look at a domestic cat you will see this shining at night.

In comparison to other *Panthera* species of the same weight, jaguars have shorter, more muscular legs, which are what give them the power they are famous for.

. . .

The size of a jaguar largely depends on which region it comes from. Generally, they increase in size from north to south, so Brazilian jaguars are larger than those living in Mexico, for example.

. . .

A footprint from a jaguar's front foot measures 10 cm (4") long and 12 cm (4.8") wide.

Female jaguar near Piquiri River in Brazil.

© Charles J. Sharp

The jaguar's coat ranges in color from a pale
yellow or tan to a reddish-brown. They have
a much paler underbelly. On their neck, body
and legs they have spots that form rosettes. In
the middle of some of these rosettes are black
dots. On their heads and underbellies, they have
simple black dots.

. . .

Jaguars that live in forests usually have darker
coats and are smaller than those living in more
open areas.

. . .

A jaguar's distinct pattern works as camouflage
in forested areas and when they're hiding in the
shadows or in caves.

Can you tell the difference between a jaguar and a leopard? Although they look similar, there are some simple differences. Jaguars have a more square head with shorter legs. They also have black dots in the middle of some of their rosettes, whereas leopards don't.

· · ·

Jaguars have very strong jaws—they have the most powerful bite of all big cat species in relation to body weight. They use their teeth to bite through the thick hides of prey such as crocodiles and turtles.

A jaguar showing us its teeth and long tongue at Toronto Zoo.

© Marcus Obal

Although jaguars are renowned for their
strength, they are also stealthy and graceful
in their movements, qualities that make them
such great hunters.

. . .

Like other cats, jaguars have sharp bumps
on their tongues, called *papillae*, which are
useful for scraping meat off bones.

. . .

Jaguars are described as **opportunistic
carnivores**, which means they only eat
meat—and aren't too fussy about what type of
meat!

Jaguar Chit-Chats

Jaguars may not talk like humans, but they have their own unique sounds to communicate with each other called **vocalisations**, which can be a combination of **grunts** and **roars**.

Like lions and tigers, jaguars have an elastic ligament behind their nose and mouth called an **epihyoideum**, which allows them to roar but not purr. In the same spot, domestic cats have a bony part, which allows them to purr, but not roar!

Both male and female jaguars can roar, but a male jaguar's roar is louder and coarser than a female's. Jaguars use their roar to scare off other jaguars, attract a mate and to defend their territory.

Yawning or roaring, what do you think? *© Yannick Turbe*

When greeting each other, or when a mother is comforting her cubs, jaguars use a sound called '**chuffing**', which is a short, low grunting sound.

One of the most common sound you'll hear a jaguar make is called a '**saw**', as it sounds like wood being sawed, but only in one direction.

Jaguar cubs also have their own sounds including **bleating, meowing** and **gurgling**.

Jaguars' Daily Lives

What's life like as a jaguar?

Jaguars are primarily **solitary**, except for females with cubs, and have their own home ranges or **territories**.

• • •

A male jaguar's territory is twice the size of a female's territory. The average female jaguar's territory is around 25-38 km^2, however, the size depends on where they live and how much prey is available.

A jaguar in its natural habitat.

Jaguars use urine, faeces and scrape marks on trees to mark their territory and let other jaguars know that that particular area is 'taken'. Male jaguars put more effort into marking their territories than females, as they want to warn off other males.

• • •

Jaguars live in a wide range of habitats, however, the most important thing for them when selecting a habitat is water supply, plenty of prey and dense vegetation so they can hide and hunt.

A female jaguar taking a rest on a tree stump.

Jaguars are a **keystone species**, which means that they play a very important role in their environment particularly when it comes to controlling prey populations. If a keystone species didn't exist, the whole environment in which it lived would be completely different.

• • •

Jaguars usually rest between the mid-morning and afternoon. They like to lie under thick vegetation, in caves or in dark shady areas. During flood seasons, they sometimes also rest in trees where it is drier.

A young male jaguar drinking at a river.

© Bernard Dupont

Although jaguars are primarily **nocturnal**, meaning they are most active during the night, their daily routine largely mimics their main prey species, in both timing and location. They mostly hunt at night, but will occasionally hunt during the day if they need to.

• • •

Jaguars *love* water! They are great swimmers and are the most water-loving of all cat species. They use the water to cool down on hot days and for hunting.

Jaguars can climb trees, but they don't do it very often. Occasionally they will drag their prey into trees to protect it from other predators. Cougars, on the other hand, love being in the trees!

In the wild, jaguars have a life span of around 8-10 years, but in captivity, this increases to 20 years.

Can you spot the jaguar camouflaged in the tree? *© Dylan Conway*

Catching Dinner:
The Jaguar Way

Jaguars are **carnivores**, meaning they only eat meat. Thankfully, they are famous for their powerful teeth and jaws that allow them to take down prey up to four times their own weight! They are **opportunistic predators**, so will often walk huge distances each day to find and catch their prey.

Unlike other big cats, jaguars kill their prey with a bite to the back of the skull rather than biting the neck or throat.

Jaguars are known for being some of the best hunters in the animal kingdom. They use a **stalk-and-ambush** hunting strategy, meaning they catch prey by stalking them and pouncing on them very quickly.